Girl Talk
Questions

Asked by Girls, Answered by You!

Published by Pleasant Company Publications

Copyright © 2006 by American Girl, LLC

Questions or comments? Call 1-800-845-0005,
visit our Web site at **americangirl.com**,
or write to Customer Service, American Girl,
8400 Fairway Place, Middleton, WI 53562-0497.

Printed in China.
06 07 08 09 10 11 LEO 10 9 8 7 6 5 4 3 2 1

Editorial Development: Therese Kauchak Maring

Art Direction & Design: Camela Decaire

Production: Mindy Rappe, Kendra Schluter, Jeannette Bailey, Judith Lary

Illustrations: Ali Douglass

Dear Reader,

Girl Talk Questions is a book **about you.** It's also a book about what other girls—from all over the country—would like to know about you!

We asked girls ages 8 to 12, "If you were sitting down with a brand-new friend, what would you want to know about her?" Some of their questions are **creative,** some are **quirky,** some are **serious,** and some are **funny.** Filling out the answers can take you on an interesting journey around—and into—your life.

Start at the beginning, or start in the middle. If you want, start at the end with the just-for-fun Silly Poll of Random Questions. When you're all done, step back and take a look at the girl you've described. We bet she sounds pretty great—just the kind of girl we'd like to be friends with!

**Sincerely,
Your friends at American Girl**

If you were describing yourself to someone, what would you say?
Emily, age 11, Texas

Are you a crafter or a noncrafter?
Emily, age 12, California

Do you have a nickname that your friends call you? If so, what is the story behind it?
Stephanie, age 12, Ohio

Do you have any collections?
Emma, age 11, New Jersey

Do you like where you live,
or would you like to live somewhere else?
Why and where?
Mikeala, age 12, Hawaii

Do you have any funny habits, like walking in your sleep or chewing on pencils?

Emily, age 11, Texas

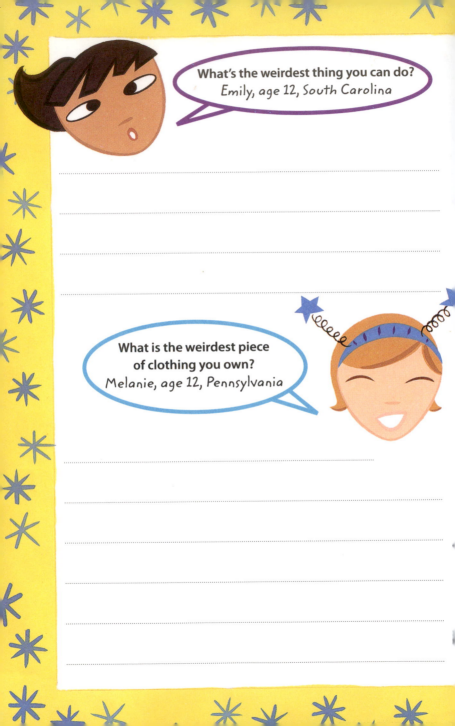

What's the weirdest thing you can do?
Emily, age 12, South Carolina

What is the weirdest piece of clothing you own?
Melanie, age 12, Pennsylvania

What are your top ten favorite hobbies?
Shanea, age 11, Wisconsin

1. ....

2. ....

3. ....

4. ....

5. ....

6. ....

7. ....

8. ....

9. ....

10. ....

Where do you see yourself in five years?
Haley, age 12, Hawaii

What do you think you will be doing in 10 years?
Sarah, age 13, Colorado

What do you see yourself doing in 20 years?
Laura, age 9, New York

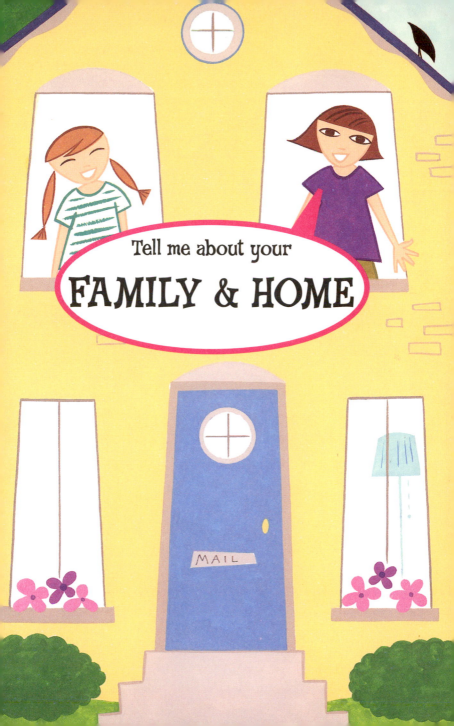

Tell me about your

FAMILY & HOME

If I were to switch places with you for a day, what would you want me to know ahead of time about your family so I could prepare?
Laila, age 13, Washington

Would you say your family is crazy or calm?
Maria, age 13, Ohio

What are your brothers and sisters like?
Avery, age 8, Ohio

Would you rather have more brothers or more sisters?
Elizabeth, age 12, Utah

Who is the funniest person in your family? Describe a funny thing that person has done.
Kinslyn, age 11, South Carolina

If you could change places with anybody in your family, who would it be?
Zoe, age 11, Colorado

When you get older, what family member do you want to be most like? Why?
Lizzie, age 10, Ohio

Can you give each person in your family a funny nickname based on personality?
Jamie, age 11, New Hampshire

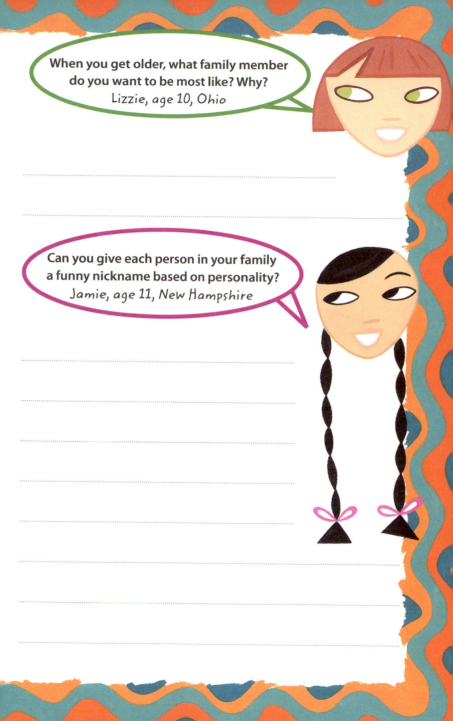

Have any family members taught you a hobby that they used to do when they were young? What is it?
Audri, age 8, Minnesota

What do you like best about your grandparents?
Danielle, age 12, New Hampshire

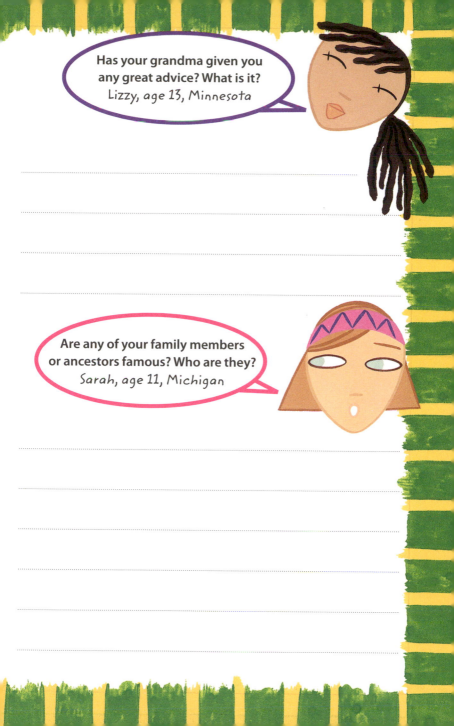

Has your grandma given you any great advice? What is it?
Lizzy, age 13, Minnesota

Are any of your family members or ancestors famous? Who are they?
Sarah, age 11, Michigan

What's the craziest thing your whole family has ever done together?
Brenn, age 9, Illinois

What silly traditions do you have in your family?
Sadie, age 11, Rhode Island

Do you have any strange holiday traditions, like leaving something funny out for Santa on Christmas Eve?
Jane, age 12, California

Is your bedroom big and open or small and cozy?
Andrea, age 11, Pennsylvania

What kind of house would you like to live in when you grow up?
Shanea, age 11, Wisconsin

What do you think your room will look like in ten years?
Lizzy, age 13, Minnesota

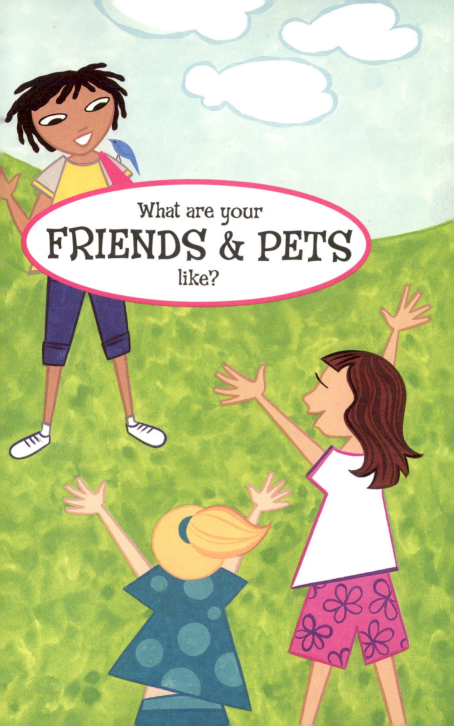

What are your
FRIENDS & PETS
like?

What do you think a good friend should be like? Should she be loyal, trustworthy . . . what else?

Marina, age 10, New Mexico

You probably have some friends you've known for years and other friends you've just recently met. What's your record for the longest amount of time you have been friends with someone? How long have you been with your newest friend?

Emma, age 13, Colorado

Would you say your friends are like your twins, totally different from you, or a mix of both?
Becky, age 12, Vermont

How did you and one of your closest friends meet?
Hannah, age 12, Oregon

What are your three favorite things about one of your friends?
Tori, age 8, Montana

What is the nicest thing a friend has done or said to you?
Brennah, age 8, Ohio

What's a kooky adventure you and your best friend have had together?
Melissa, age 12, Tennessee

Has a friend ever helped
you overcome something hard? How?
Peach, age 11, Massachusetts

What kind of pets do you have or would you like to have?
Adia, age 8, New York

Have you ever had a pet that ran away? What happened?
Lucy, age 8, Georgia

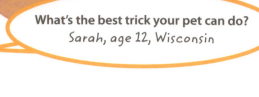

What's the best trick your pet can do?
Sarah, age 12, Wisconsin

Have you ever done something special to remember a pet you don't have anymore?
Lori, age 9, Texas

What is the funniest pet name you've heard of?
Morgan Marie, age 8, New York

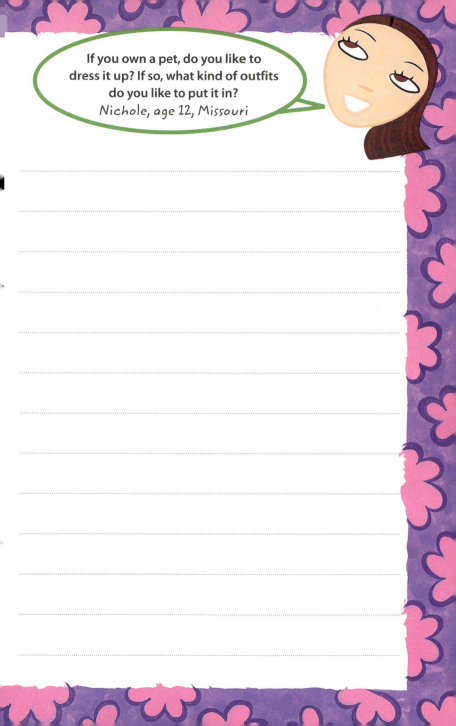

If you own a pet, do you like to dress it up? If so, what kind of outfits do you like to put it in?
Nichole, age 12, Missouri

If you could meet anyone in the world, who would it be?
Hannah, age 8, Wisconsin

Which character in a book or movie do you think you are like?
Eugenia, age 9, New York

Which kind of movies do you like better—scary ones or comedies?
Shelby, age 12, Tennessee

What is the best gift you've ever made for someone?
Claire, age 8, Connecticut

What is the oddest gift you ever received?
Emma, age 8, Massachusetts

Has there ever been a moment when you couldn't stop laughing? What happened?
Erin, age 10, Wisconsin

If you could go back in time, how would you prevent your most embarrassing moment from happening?
Ashley, age 13, Tennessee

What was the greatest April Fools' prank you ever pulled—or had pulled on you?
Shubha, age 10, Arizona

For Halloween, do you like to be scaaaaaaaaaary or cute?
Portland Pal, age 11, Oregon

Have you ever had a serious talk with your mom? How did it go?
Hannah, age 12, Massachusetts

What is the funniest thing that has ever happened to you?
Sydney, age 10, Kentucky

Have you ever had a dream that you don't think you will ever forget? Why will it stick in your memory?
Caroline, age 12, Utah

Have you ever had a dream about something and then had it really happen?
Brenna, age 9, Illinois

Have you ever had the same dream more than once? What was it about?

Tina, age 12, Minnesota

If you could invent something that would help the planet, what would you invent?
Sarah, age 12, Wisconsin

Are there any laws that you would like to change?
Tori, age 11, California

Are you scared of anything unusual, like chickens?
Jina, age 11, Virginia

Can you think of fake scientific names for some things that you're afraid of? For example, if you're afraid of grasshoppers, you could call it *hopiphobia*.
American Idol fan, age 13, Wisconsin

When you were little, what did you imagine the monsters under your bed looked like?

Lizzy, age 13, Minnesota

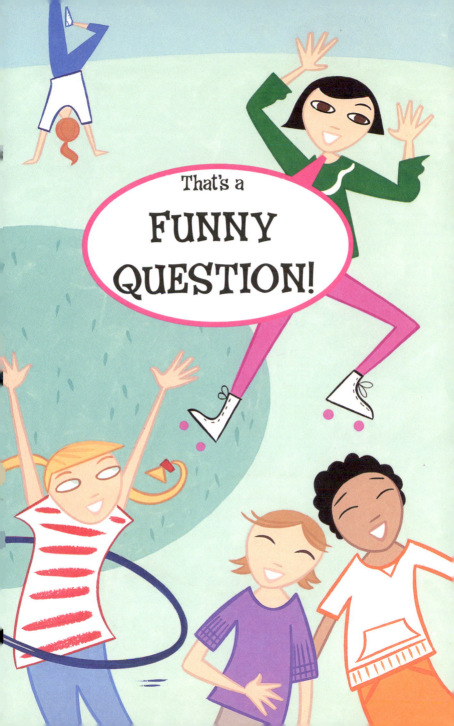

Would you rather get in a whipped-cream fight or a chocolate-syrup fight?
Anna, age 12, Wyoming

What is the weirdest food combination that you like to eat?
Erin, age 10, Wisconsin

MILK
SODA

Which would you rather do live in front of ten billion people: disco dance to Elvis Presley music or hula to tropical music?
Anna, age 10, California

What songs do you sing in the shower?
Elizabeth, age 12, New York

What song do you dance around to in your bedroom the most?
Maddie, age 12, New York

What is the funkiest dance you can do?
Kate, age 10, Florida

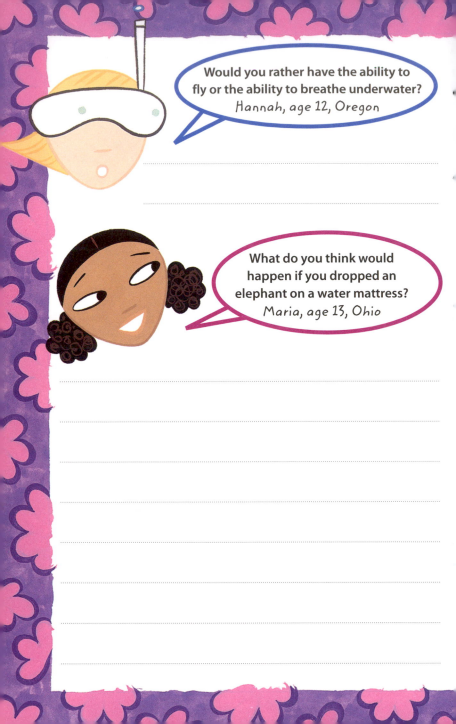

Would you rather have the ability to fly or the ability to breathe underwater?
Hannah, age 12, Oregon

What do you think would happen if you dropped an elephant on a water mattress?
Maria, age 13, Ohio

If you were to reach down under a chair and touch a huge spiderweb, what would your first reaction be?
Marie, age 12, West Virginia

What's the weirdest thing you've ever found at the back of your closet or under your bed?
Madelyn, age 13, Washington

Which would you rather wear in public—a feather boa or a floppy hat that's two sizes too big?
Audrey, age 13, Ohio

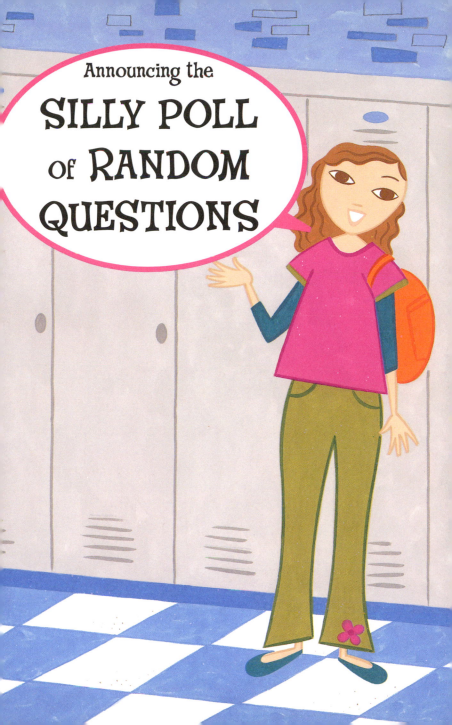

American girls want to know your answers to these silly yes-or-no questions. Mark the box next to each question.

Have you ever worn your slippers to school?

Jennie, age 8, Ohio

❑ YES   ❑ NO

Can you say a tongue twister 20 times fast?
Sarah, age 9, Kentucky

❑ YES   ❑ NO

Do people really slip on banana peels?
Meredith, age 10, Kentucky

❑ YES   ❑ NO

Have you ever accidentally worn your shirt backwards?
Mallory, age 10, California

❑ YES   ❑ NO

Do you like Brussels sprouts?
Marina, age 10, New Mexico

❑ YES   ❑ NO

Have you ever dropped something really important into a cafeteria trash can?
Emma, age 10, Kansas

❑ YES   ❑ NO

Have you fallen into a lake?
Samantha, age 11, Wisconsin

❑ YES   ❑ NO

Do you like macaroni and ketchup together?
Cici, age 11, Colorado

❑ YES   ❑ NO

Do you like llamas?
Zina, age 11, Illinois

❑ YES   ❑ NO

Do you collect toy mice?
Kinslyn, age 11, South Carolina

❑ YES   ❑ NO

Would you ever dive into a pool of Jell-O?
Shelly, age 12, Connecticut

❑ YES   ❑ NO

Have you ever tried to brush a dog's teeth?
Chelsea, age 12, Virginia

❑ YES   ❑ NO

Do you like steamed broccoli?
Melissa, age 12, Tennessee

❑ YES   ❑ NO

Have you ever imagined life as a pet parakeet?
Katie, age 12, New York

❑   YES   ❑ NO

**Has your belly button ever changed from an "innie"
to an "outtie," or from an "outtie" to an "innie"?**
Altair, age 12, Montana

❑ YES   ❑ NO

Have you ever ridden a camel?
Allison, age 12, North Carolina

❑ YES   ❑ NO

Do you ever wish you were a hippo?
Savannah, age 12, New Jersey

❏ YES   ❏ NO

Are you a good hula hoop-er?
Morgan, age 12, Minnesota

❏ YES   ❏ NO

Have you ever wondered if a dolphin has body odor?
Elizabeth, age 12, Utah

❏ YES   ❏ NO

Do you sleep with a purple stuffed gorilla at night?
Miriam, age 12, Minnesota

❏ YES   ❏ NO

Do you make faces at yourself in the mirror?
Elizabeth, age 12, North Carolina

❏ YES   ❏ NO

Have you ever worn a wig just for the heck of it?
Maddie, age 12, Texas

❏ YES   ❏ NO

Do you like cheese?
Optimistic in Ohio, age 13, Ohio

❑ YES   ❑ NO

Have you ever called anyone besides your mom "Mom"?
Linnea, age 13, California

❑ YES   ❑ NO

Have you ever laughed so hard, you had milk come out your nose?
Katelyn, age 13, Tennessee

❑ YES   ❑ NO

Do you know anyone who has a pet pig?
Sara, age 13, Michigan

❑ YES   ❑ NO

Would you like more
Girl Talk Questions?

What would **you** like
to ask other girls?

Send your ideas to:

Girl Talk Questions Editor
American Girl
8400 Fairway Place
Middleton, WI 53562

All comments and suggestions received
by American Girl may be used without
compensation or acknowledgment.
Sorry, photos can't be returned.

Here are some other American Girl books you might like:

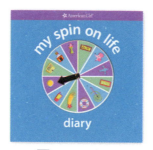

❑ I read it.

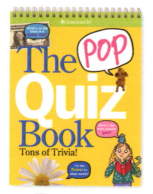

❑ I read it.

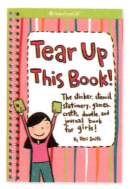

❑ I read it.